WORDS THAT SHAPED AMERICA

THE MOST POWERFUL WORDS OF THE CIVIL WAR

FOUR SCORE AND SEVEN YEARS AGO OUR FATHERS BROUGHT FORTH ON THIS CONTINENT A NEW NATION CONCEIVED IN LIBERTY AND DEDICATED TO THE PROPOSITION THAT ALL MEN ARE CREATED EQUAL

BY JASON GLASER

Gareth Stevens PUBLISHING

Please visit our website, www.garethstevens.com. For a free color catalog of all our high-quality books, call toll free 1-800-542-2595 or fax 1-877-542-2596.

Library of Congress Cataloging-in-Publication Data

Names: Glaser, Jason, author. | Wright, John D., 1938-
Title: The most powerful words of the Civil War / Jason Glaser.
Description: New York : Gareth Stevens Publishing, 2020. | Series: Words that shaped america | Includes index.
Identifiers: LCCN 2019030744 | ISBN 9781538248164 | ISBN 9781538248171 (library binding) | ISBN 9781538248157 (paperback) | ISBN 9781538248188 (ebook)
Subjects: LCSH: United States--History--Civil War, 1861-1865--Quotations. | United States--History--Civil War, 1861-1865--Juvenile literature.
Classification: LCC E468.9 .G65 2020 | DDC 973.7--dc23
LC record available at https://lccn.loc.gov/2019030744

First Edition

Published in 2020 by
Gareth Stevens Publishing
111 East 14th Street, Suite 349
New York, NY 10003

Designer: Sarah Liddell
Editor: Therese Shea

Photo credits: Cover, p. 1 (main) US National Archives bot/Wikimedia Commons; cover, p. 1 (inset) Theomamentalist/Wikimedia Commons; ink smear used throughout Itsmesimon/Shutterstock.com; border used throughout igorrita/Shutterstock.com; background used throughout Lukasz Szwaj/Shutterstock.com; p. 5 (Constitution) Earthsound/Wikimedia Commons; p. 5 (Declaration of Independence) Parhamr/Wikimedia Commons; p. 7 (Frederick Douglass) Fastfission~commonswiki/Wikimedia Commons; p. 7 (Harriet Tubman) Scewing/Wikimedia Commons; p. 9 (Lucretia Mott) Jan Arkestejn/Wikimedia Commons; p. 9 (Brooks and Sumner) Fotosearch/Stringer/Archive Photos/Getty Images; pp. 11, 13 Bettmann/Contributor/Bettmann/Getty Images; p. 14 Chicago History Museum/Contributor/Archive Photos/Getty Images; p. 15 Picturenow/Contributor/Universal Images Group/Getty Images; pp. 16, 22 Fæ/Wikimedia Commons; p. 17 Fine Art/Contributor/Corbis Historical/Getty Images; p. 19 Gamaliel/Wikimedia Commons; p. 21 Library of Congress/Archive Photos/Getty Images; p. 23 Pufacz/Wikimedia Commons; p. 25 Howcheng/Wikimedia Commons; p. 27 John Dominis/Contributor/The LIFE Picture Collection/Getty Images.

Printed in the United States of America

CPSIA compliance information: Batch #CW20GS: For further information contact Gareth Stevens, New York, New York at 1-800-542-2595.

CONTENTS

Words in the glossary appear in **bold** type the first time they are used in the text.

FOUNDATIONS OF FREEDOM

In 1776, the Declaration of Independence stated: "We hold these truths to be self-evident, that all men are created equal." This bold statement also identified "**unalienable** Rights" for Americans, explaining that "among these are life, liberty, and the pursuit of happiness."

However, freedom and equality didn't extend to slaves. In fact, the US Constitution said that slaves were to be counted as just "three fifths of all other Persons." And when the Bill of Rights was added to the Constitution, it closed by saying additional powers are "reserved" for the states and for US citizens. However, this meant that states could permit slavery. The young country became divided along the lines of slavery. War became unavoidable. Powerful words spoken and written by people on each side teach about this difficult time in the nation's history.

BEHIND THE WORDS

THE FIRST AFRICAN SLAVES ARRIVED IN THE AMERICAN COLONIES IN 1619.

THE POWER OF REPRESENTATION

A state's population determines its number of representatives in Congress. Southern states wanted slaves included in the population count, so they could have as much political power as Northern states. It was decided that three-fifths of the population of slaves would be considered as part of a whole population. The Three-Fifths Compromise allowed states with slavery to have power in Congress, but not as much as if slaves were counted as white citizens.

DECLARATION OF INDEPENDENCE

US CONSTITUTION

THE DECLARATION OF INDEPENDENCE AND THE US CONSTITUTION ARE AMONG THE NATION'S MOST PRIZED DOCUMENTS, YET THESE POWERFUL WORDS OF FREEDOM DIDN'T EXTEND TO AMERICAN SLAVES.

RISE OF THE ABOLITIONISTS

The cause of abolition, or the ending of slavery, was more popular in Northern states, which relied less on slave labor. States and territories in the South and West had economies built around farming and were more dependent on slave labor. Abolitionists were those who worked against slavery, even helping slaves escape.

One abolitionist was a former slave named Frederick Douglass. He began his own newspaper called *The North Star*. He spoke out not just against slavery but also to seek full equality under the law for black people. Douglass said, "We ask that in our native land, we shall not be treated as strangers, and worse than strangers." His powerful plea reminded people that black Americans were being treated terribly in their own country.

BEHIND THE WORDS

FREDERICK DOUGLASS NAMED HIS PAPER AFTER THE REAL NORTH STAR, WHICH HELPED GUIDE RUNAWAY SLAVES NORTH. "TO THOUSANDS NOW FREE . . . IT HAS BEEN THE STAR OF FREEDOM," HE SAID.

THE UNDERGROUND RAILROAD WAS THE NETWORK OF ROUTES THAT HELPED SLAVES REACH FREEDOM. ITS MOST FAMOUS GUIDE WAS HARRIET TUBMAN. SHE HELPED FREE DOZENS, IF NOT HUNDREDS, OF SLAVES.

HARRIET TUBMAN

FREDERICK DOUGLASS

SONGS OF FREEDOM

Slave owners probably thought that slaves singing as they worked were trying to keep their spirits up. The songs are known as spirituals. But when slaves sang out certain songs, it was a code. For example, singing "Swing Low, Sweet Chariot" let slaves know that someone was coming to help them escape to freedom. Other songs told slaves exactly how to escape. These moving songs, still sung today, connect Americans to their ancestors' struggles.

A NATION ON THE EDGE

In 1837, Southern politician John C. Calhoun warned that Northerners were turning hostile not only to slaveholders, but to people who approved of using slave labor. Northerners were becoming "taught to hate the people and institutions of nearly one half of this **Union**," he said. In fact, the "hate" was seen and heard on both sides, even in the halls of Congress. There, in 1856, a congressman from South Carolina nearly beat an abolitionist senator to death with a cane.

BEHIND THE WORDS

EVEN PROSLAVERY CITIZENS UNDERSTOOD THAT THE WORD "SLAVERY" SOUNDED BAD. THEY SOMETIMES USED SOFTER LANGUAGE. FOR INSTANCE, JOHN CALHOUN CALLED SLAVERY "THE PECULIAR INSTITUTION."

Fighting erupted all across the country, especially in places that hadn't yet determined whether to allow slavery. Groups of proslavery and antislavery Americans hoped to influence that decision. They attacked, threatened, and even killed each other to gain the upper hand.

WOMEN WEIGH IN

Despite not being allowed to vote or hold office, women had influential voices calling for change. **Activist** Angelina Grimké Weld fought against the idea that oppressed people were content with their lives. "I have never seen a happy slave," she said. Lucretia Mott, a women's rights leader, vowed to fight "injustice inflicted either on me or on the slave. I will oppose it with all the moral powers with which I am **endowed**."

LUCRETIA MOTT

REPRESENTATIVE PRESTON BROOKS OF SOUTH CAROLINA BEAT SENATOR CHARLES SUMNER OF MASSACHUSETTS OVER REMARKS AGAINST PROSLAVERY LEGISLATION. IT TOOK 3 YEARS FOR SUMNER TO FULLY RECOVER.

SUPREME INJUSTICE

If the slaves were to be free in the United States, laws that labeled them as property had to change. Abolitionist lawyers took up slaves' cases, hoping to win their freedom in court.

One slave, Dred Scott, argued that since he had lived for a time in a free state and territory, he should be freed, even in the slave state of Missouri. The case moved to the US Supreme Court. In 1857, Chief Justice Roger Taney wrote: "Dred Scott was not a citizen of Missouri within the meaning of the Constitution of the United States, and not entitled as such to sue [for his freedom]." The ruling extended slavery into free states and territories and meant that African Americans were not and could not be US citizens.

BEHIND THE WORDS

IN 1868, THE FOURTEENTH AMENDMENT TO THE CONSTITUTION FINALLY GRANTED CITIZENSHIP TO ALL AFRICAN AMERICANS.

RUNAWAY RIGHTS

As more free states and territories joined the United States, slave states began to feel outnumbered. They pushed for stronger laws to protect slavery. The Fugitive Slave Act of 1850 required that people in free states and territories return slaves found there back to their owners: "All good citizens are hereby commanded to aid and assist . . . whenever their services may be required." Escaping to the North no longer meant freedom for slaves.

DRED SCOTT

A PAINTING OF DRED SCOTT IN THE MISSOURI HISTORICAL SOCIETY REMINDS PEOPLE TODAY THAT A MISSOURI JURY RULED SCOTT FREE. HIS OWNER CHALLENGED THE DECISION, WHICH IS WHY THE CASE WENT TO THE US SUPREME COURT.

THE GREAT DEBATES

The United States was still a growing nation in the mid-1800s. Before the 1858 election, Stephen Douglas, a senator from Illinois, and challenger Abraham Lincoln held a series of **debates** about allowing slavery in newly formed states. Their positions mirrored the divisions of the country.

Douglas argued that each state had the right to decide for itself whether to allow slavery. He maintained, "It is none of your business in Missouri whether Kansas shall adopt slavery or reject it. It is the business of her people and none of yours."

BEHIND THE WORDS

FOR EACH DEBATE, DOUGLAS OR LINCOLN SPOKE FOR AN HOUR BEFORE ALLOWING AN HOUR AND A HALF FOR THE OPPONENT TO REPLY. THEN, THE FIRST SPEAKER GOT ANOTHER HALF HOUR TO RESPOND.

Lincoln argued the country couldn't remain divided on slavery. "A house divided against itself cannot stand," he said, quoting the Bible. All states should allow slavery or all should be free, according to Lincoln.

People all over the country read about the debates in newspapers. "The battle of the Union is to be fought in Illinois," one newspaper claimed. Although Douglas won the Senate election, the debates made Lincoln famous.

THE KANSAS-NEBRASKA ACT

The US government had tried to keep peace for years by making laws that attempted to maintain a balance between the slave states and the free states. However, the Kansas-Nebraska Act, which Stephen Douglas first introduced in 1854, didn't require that balance. It moved the fight over slavery out of Washington, DC, and put it on the public's shoulders. It gave the people of new states the power to decide whether they would allow slavery within their borders.

BREAKING AWAY

In 1860, Abraham Lincoln ran for president as a Republican. The Republican Party had formed to oppose slavery in US territories, so opponents believed Lincoln would end slavery. When Lincoln won the election, Southern states already had plans for **secession**.

The first to leave the Union was South Carolina in December 1860. The state's letter of secession declared: "A geographical line has been drawn across the Union, and all the States north of that line have united in the election of a man to the high office of President of the United States, whose opinions and purposes are hostile to slavery." Other Southern states followed South Carolina, forming the Confederate States of America. The first fighting of the Civil War occurred in April 1861 at Fort Sumter in South Carolina.

CHARLESTON
MERCURY
EXTRA:
Passed unanimously at 1.15 o'clock, P. M., December 20th, 1860.
AN ORDINANCE
To dissolve the Union between the State of South Carolina and other States united with her under the compact entitled "The Constitution of the United States of America."
THE
UNION
IS
DISSOLVED!

DRAFT OPPOSITION

The Union and Confederate armies depended on volunteers at first. As the Civil War dragged on, both the Union and the Confederacy instituted **drafts**, which angered many citizens. Then, in 1863, a federal law allowed people who could afford it to avoid serving in the military by giving the government money or by paying someone else to serve in their place. This caused a **riot** in New York City, and at least 120 people were killed over 5 days.

FORT SUMTER WAS A FEDERAL FORT IN SOUTH CAROLINA. ON APRIL 12, 1861, CONFEDERATE SOLDIERS BEGAN TO FIRE ON THE FORT, EVENTUALLY FORCING UNION TROOPS TO LEAVE.

BEHIND THE WORDS

IN LINCOLN'S FIRST ADDRESS AS PRESIDENT, HE SAID, "I HAVE NO PURPOSE, DIRECTLY OR INDIRECTLY, TO INTERFERE WITH THE INSTITUTION OF SLAVERY IN THE STATES WHERE IT EXISTS." YET, THE SECEDED STATES REFUSED TO REJOIN THE UNION.

THE EMANCIPATION PROCLAMATION

In September 1862, Abraham Lincoln issued a powerful statement, the Emancipation Proclamation, which was a promise to slaves behind Confederate lines. As of January 1, 1863, "all persons held as slaves within said **designated** States, and parts of States, are, and henceforward [from now on] shall be free." Emancipating, or freeing, slaves gave the Union soldiers another cause to fight for. However, the Emancipation Proclamation didn't free slaves in places already captured by the Union army. Total abolition wouldn't happen until the Thirteenth Amendment to the Constitution became law in 1865.

Also in the proclamation, Lincoln, as the commander in chief of the US military, declared slaves from the Confederacy could join the Union army. About 180,000 black soldiers fought for the Union army by the end of the war.

EMANCIPATION PROCLAMATION

WAR OF WORDS

Newspapers in the North and South tried to inspire men to fight and encourage hatred of the enemy. Southern papers described Lincoln as a bloodthirsty tyrant who would destroy their homes. A paper in Richmond, Virginia, wrote, "The invaders are upon you." "They come to butcher and enslave." A Cleveland, Ohio, paper described Confederate soldiers as savage fighters who "severed the heads of our dead from their bodies, and amused themselves by kicking them about as footballs."

BATTLE OF ANTIETAM

FIVE DAYS BEFORE LINCOLN ISSUED THE EMANCIPATION PROCLAMATION, THE UNION WON A HARD-FOUGHT VICTORY AT THE BATTLE OF ANTIETAM IN MARYLAND. THE CONFEDERATES LOST 13,724 TROOPS, AND THE UNION LOST 12,410.

BEHIND THE WORDS

LINCOLN LATER SAID THE EMANCIPATION PROCLAMATION WAS "THE CENTRAL ACT OF MY **ADMINISTRATION**, AND THE GREATEST EVENT OF THE NINETEENTH CENTURY."

ON THE BATTLEFIELD

Confederate officer Nathan Bedford Forrest famously said, "War means fighting, and fighting means killing." Some of the most powerful Civil War stories come from the ordinary soldiers who were doing the fighting.

BEHIND THE WORDS

UNION GENERAL ULYSSES S. GRANT LED THE CAPTURING OF VICKSBURG, MISSISSIPPI, WHICH OCCURRED JULY 4, 1863. HE SAID, "THE ENTIRE **REBEL** FORCE HERETOFORE [UP UNTIL NOW] AGAINST ME ARE COMPLETELY AT MY MERCY."

In July 1863, the Confederate and Union forces met at Gettysburg, Pennsylvania. A Confederate soldier recalled an extraordinary meeting with a Union soldier after being shot: "I called to him for help. Coming up, he said: 'Put your arm around my neck and throw all your weight on me; don't be afraid of me. Hurry up; this is a dangerous place.' . . . He said: 'If you and I had this matter to settle, we would soon settle it, wouldn't we?'" This encounter suggests that whether Confederate or Union, most soldiers were just trying to survive the most deadly war in US history.

CONFEDERATE VICTORIES, UNION DEFEATS

The strength of the Confederate army had surprised the Union at first. Confederate forces won major battles in the first years of the war, such as the First and Second Battles of Bull Run in 1861 and 1862. Under General Robert E. Lee, the Confederates also defeated the Union forces at Fredericksburg, Virginia, in 1862, with heavy **casualties**. Lee said, "It is well that war is so terrible, or we would grow too fond of it."

THE BATTLE OF GETTYSBURG, A UNION VICTORY, WAS CONSIDERED A TURNING POINT OF THE WAR. IT WAS ALSO THE BLOODIEST BATTLE OF THE WAR.

THE GETTYSBURG ADDRESS

The Union victory at Gettysburg stopped the Confederate invasion into the North. The cost of victory was high. Over 7,000 Union and Confederate soldiers were killed over 3 days of fighting. Thousands more were wounded.

BEHIND THE WORDS

AT THE GETTYSBURG CEREMONY, LINCOLN SAID, "THE WORLD WILL LITTLE NOTE NOR LONG REMEMBER WHAT WE SAY HERE." HIS ADDRESS, ONLY 272 WORDS LONG, IS ONE OF THE MOST WELL KNOWN IN US HISTORY.

Four months later, at a ceremony to **dedicate** a cemetery in Gettysburg, President Lincoln delivered a memorable speech: the Gettysburg Address. Inspired by the Declaration of Independence, which had been approved "four score and seven years" (or 87 years) before, Lincoln reminded listeners that the nation was "dedicated to the proposition [idea] that all men are created equal." On behalf of the fallen soldiers, he said, "We have come to dedicate a portion of that field as a final resting place for those who gave their lives that that nation might live."

FOR THE UNION DEAD

Abraham Lincoln's speech honored the Union soldiers who had fought and died there, and the new cemetery was meant for them. After the Battle of Gettysburg, fallen soldiers had been hurriedly buried in shallow graves with simple markers. It was decided to rebury the Union soldiers in a nearby national cemetery. Beginning in the 1870s, about 3,200 Confederate soldiers were reburied in Southern states. Some still remain under the battlefields of Gettysburg, however.

A LARGE CROWD GATHERED AT THE DEDICATION OF THE GETTYSBURG NATIONAL CEMETERY ON NOVEMBER 19, 1863.

LETTERS FROM HOME

Most Civil War soldiers could read and write. Many regularly wrote letters home. The letters they received encouraged and informed them about life at home. "Duty, discipline, everything, at once gives way to the reading of the letters," wrote Union officer Charles Francis Adams Jr., describing the letters' importance.

As the war stretched on, hardships grew across the nation. Some soldiers' families begged them to come home. A Confederate soldier received a letter that said: "Edward, your darling Lucy; she never complains but she is growing thinner and thinner every day. And before God, Edward, unless you come home, we must die." Such powerful pleas caused soldiers to desert the army. By fall 1864, the Confederate army was severely weakened by desertions. By 1865, whole camps were going home.

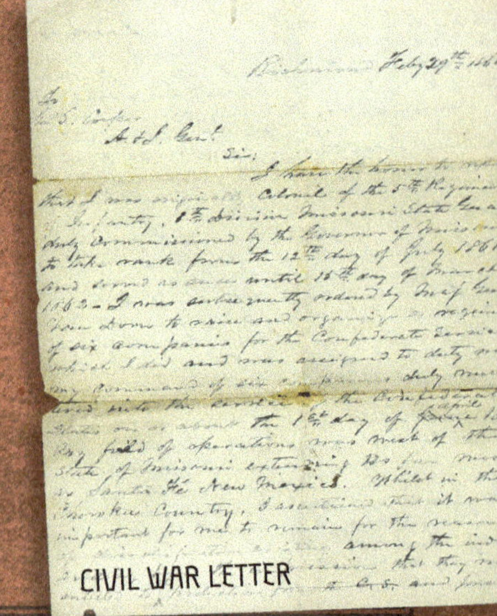

CIVIL WAR LETTER

ATLANTA BURNS

In March 1864, Union general William Tecumseh Sherman marched south from Tennessee to Atlanta, Georgia. Atlanta fell to Union forces in September 1864. More than one-third of the city was destroyed before they left in November. Sherman stated, "Behind us lay Atlanta smoldering [burning] and in ruins, the black smoke rising high in the air and hanging like a pall [dark covering] over the ruined city." Another Union soldier wrote, "We have utterly destroyed Atlanta."

SOME CIVIL WAR SOLDIERS CARRIED LETTERS IN THEIR POCKETS THAT WERE MEANT FOR THEIR LOVED ONES IN CASE THEY DIED ON THE BATTLEFIELD.

BEHIND THE WORDS

THE UNITED STATES BANNED THE NORMAL EXCHANGE OF MAIL BETWEEN THE NORTH AND SOUTH IN AUGUST 1861. HOWEVER, THERE WAS A SPECIAL SYSTEM TO SEND LETTERS, THOUGH THEY HAD TO BE APPROVED FIRST.

SURRENDER AND REUNITING

A lack of soldiers, food, and supplies in addition to mounting defeats took a toll on the Confederate army. Surrounded and outnumbered, Confederate general Robert E. Lee surrendered on April 9, 1865, at Appomattox Court House, Virginia. Lee was the leader of the Confederate army at that point. His surrender marked the beginning of the end for the Confederacy. Union general Ulysses S. Grant set the terms of surrender.

Grant promised, "Each officer and man will be allowed to return to his home, not to be disturbed by United States authority." He allowed Confederate soldiers to keep some of their horses and guns. He also informed Union soldiers "the Rebels are our countrymen again" and encouraged them to celebrate the end of the war, not the defeat of fellow Americans.

BEHIND THE WORDS

MANY IN THE NORTH WANTED ROBERT E. LEE AND OTHER SOLDIERS TRIED FOR TREASON, BUT ULYSSES S. GRANT THREATENED TO RESIGN IF THAT HAPPENED.

Union General William T. Sherman said, "War is cruelty. There is no use trying to reform it. The crueler it is, the sooner it will be over."

March to the Sea

The March to the Sea

After capturing Atlanta, General William T. Sherman led Union troops southeast across the state of Georgia to the coast in November 1864. This was the Union army's "March to the Sea." They destroyed anything that could be helpful to the Confederate army on the way. In December 1864, Sherman sent Lincoln a message that read: "I beg to present you as a Christmas gift the city of Savannah." The Union had captured another Southern city.

AFTER EMANCIPATION

After the war, it took years to rebuild the South and reestablish trust between the Union and the former Confederacy. Yet little was done to help former slaves. The newspaper *Weekly Anglo-African* recognized the danger: "To be sure, there will be no actual slavery, but the odor of slavocracy will be left behind with unlimited power to enact laws to suit itself."

BEHIND THE WORDS

THE US GOVERNMENT COLLECTED JAMES JOHNSON'S EXPERIENCES AND OTHER FREED SLAVES' LIFE STORIES AS PART OF THE FEDERAL WRITERS' PROJECT IN THE 1930s.

James Johnson, a freed slave from Columbia, South Carolina, thought the years after the war seemed more difficult. He recalled at least slaves had "a place to lie down at night and somewhere to eat, when they got hungry in slavery time." Despite federal laws that promised civil rights, some state and local laws kept blacks from enjoying civil rights that whites had. It would take decades before those rights were guaranteed.

A SYSTEM CALLED SHARECROPPING KEPT MANY SOUTHERN BLACKS IN POVERTY. AS SHARECROPPERS, THEY GAVE LANDOWNERS PART OF THEIR CROP AS A KIND OF RENT FOR THE LAND THEY USED.

THE ORIGINS OF JUNETEENTH

Even though the Emancipation Proclamation had freed slaves in Confederate territory in 1863, slaves often didn't know it. On June 19, 1865, Union soldiers arrived in Galveston, Texas, and informed blacks there that "all slaves are free. This involves an absolute equality of personal rights and rights of property between former masters and slaves." Each year since then, June 19 is celebrated in many places around the world as a holiday called Juneteenth.

RISING UP AGAIN?

In the years following the American Civil War, a saying emerged that's sometimes used today: "The South shall rise again." To some, the phrase means that the spirit of the Southern people can overcome hardship. Others, however, think of it as a sort of warning about the South challenging the Union once more.

BEHIND THE WORDS

A COLD WAR IS A CONFLICT IN WHICH HOSTILITIES CAUSE GREAT TENSION, BUT STOP SHORT OF OPEN WAR.

Some say the United States is in a "Civil Cold War" along political lines instead of state lines. In a few cases, this charged environment has led to fighting and even deaths. Historians have pointed out similarities between what people say and do today with the way people behaved around the time of the Civil War. Being able to recognize these patterns might keep the country from falling back into terrible violence.

HERITAGE OR HATE?

Some Confederate symbols remain in the nation today. Statues of Confederate heroes such as Robert E. Lee stand in Southern states. Some citizens openly display Confederate battle flags. Supporters argue these items are meaningful for remembering the past. Critics argue that such displays are disrespectful toward Americans whose ancestors were slaves. Protests have caused some symbols to be removed or replaced. In other cases, communities have chosen to keep them in place.

A NATION DIVIDED BY SLAVERY

1787: THE US CONSTITUTION, INCLUDING THE THREE-FIFTHS COMPROMISE, IS SIGNED.

1791: THE BILL OF RIGHTS GIVES STATES THE POWER TO ALLOW SLAVERY.

1850: HARRIET TUBMAN MAKES HER FIRST TRIP ON THE UNDERGROUND RAILROAD. THE FUGITIVE SLAVE ACT IS PASSED.

1857: DRED SCOTT LOSES HIS CASE FOR FREEDOM BEFORE THE SUPREME COURT.

1858: ABRAHAM LINCOLN AND STEPHEN DOUGLAS HOLD DEBATES ABOUT SLAVERY.

1860: LINCOLN IS ELECTED PRESIDENT. SOUTH CAROLINA IS THE FIRST STATE TO LEAVE THE UNION.

1861: THE CONFEDERACY IS FORMED BY SECEDED STATES. THE CIVIL WAR BEGINS AT FORT SUMTER.

1862: LINCOLN ISSUES THE EMANCIPATION PROCLAMATION.

1863: THE EMANCIPATION PROCLAMATION TAKES EFFECT. LINCOLN GIVES THE GETTYSBURG ADDRESS.

1864: UNION GENERAL WILLIAM T. SHERMAN CAPTURES ATLANTA AND LEADS THE MARCH TO THE SEA.

1865: ROBERT E. LEE SURRENDERS IN APRIL, AND THE CIVIL WAR ENDS IN MAY. THE THIRTEENTH AMENDMENT IS PASSED, ABOLISHING SLAVERY.

GLOSSARY

activist: one who uses or supports strong actions to help make changes in politics or society

administration: a term of office

casualty: a person who is hurt or killed during a war

debate: a formal public discussion or argument

dedicate: to open to public use. Also, to devote or commit oneself to a cause.

designated: officially chosen to do something

draft: a system in which people are required to join the armed forces of a country for a time

endowed: naturally provided with

rebel: one who fights to overthrow a government

riot: a public disturbance during which a group of angry people become noisy and out of control

secession: the act of separating from a nation and becoming independent

unalienable: not capable of being taken away

Union: the United States of America. Also, the side of the Northern states in the American Civil War.

FOR MORE INFORMATION

BOOKS

Hedtke, James R. *American Civil War: Facts and Fictions.* Santa Barbara, CA: ABC-CLIO, 2018.

Howse, Jennifer. *Reconstruction.* New York, NY: AV2 by Weigl, 2014.

Jones, Viola, and Philip Wolny. *A Primary Source Investigation of the Underground Railroad.* New York, NY: Rosen Central, 2015.

WEBSITES

Kids in the Civil War
www.pbs.org/wgbh/americanexperience/features/grant-kids/
This page discusses the Civil War from the viewpoint of children and young soldiers.

The Civil War
www.loc.gov/teachers/classroommaterials/themes/civil-war/students.html
This collection of online resources is drawn from materials kept in the Library of Congress.

INDEX